# One Man's Life In Spoken Words

## Volume I

Paul Wesley Smalls

Copyright © 2025 by Paul Wesley Smalls

All rights reserved. No part of this publication may be reproduced, distributed, or transmitted in any form or by any means, including photocopying, recording, or other electronic or mechanical methods, without the prior written permission of the publisher, except in the case of brief quotations embodied in critical reviews and certain other noncommercial uses permitted by copyright law.

# Dedication

To my father and mother, whose unwavering love and guidance have shaped my journey. I will always cherish the birthday card my father gave me, enclosing a penny with the challenge to make it grow — an enduring lesson in ambition and perseverance. His wisdom continues to inspire me to be proactive and intentional in life.

Equally, my mother's steadfast encouragement and belief in me have been a source of strength. Her words, always sincere, meant the world to me. Their faith and resilience have instilled in me the courage to pursue my dreams and strive to be the best version of myself.

# Acknowledgment

First and foremost, I give thanks to God for shaping my path and instilling in me the conviction to love and serve others.

I extend my deepest gratitude to my brother-in-law, Rick Hilke, for embracing my vision and crafting the initial design of my book cover.

A heartfelt thank you to Sharmara Rose and the Universal Book Publishing editing team for their expertise and dedication in bringing my words to life.

Finally, to my wife — your patience, support, and unwavering belief in me have been invaluable throughout this journey. This book, the realization of a lifelong dream, would not have been possible without you.

# Table of Contents

**Chapter One Personal Reflection** ........................................................... 1

Hurt Beyond Words ............................................................................. 1

In Weakness ......................................................................................... 4

Criticism At Close Range ................................................................... 6

Impulse ............................................................................................... 10

The Wall ............................................................................................. 12

Risk It All ........................................................................................... 15

The Mystery Man ............................................................................... 17

The Hardest Path ............................................................................... 19

The Uncertainty of Everything ......................................................... 21

Forever ............................................................................................... 23

**Chapter Two Imaginary Expression** ....................................................... 26

Good Tree, Bad Tree ......................................................................... 26

I Saw Two Dragons ........................................................................... 29

Dark Eyes ........................................................................................... 33

The Fierce, Tenacious, and Ordinary ............................................... 37

Worthy ............................................................................................... 43

The Mother, Father, and Wife ........................................................... 47

The Foe Living Within ...................................................................... 52

The Crumbs of Life .................................................................... 54

A Wild Horse ............................................................................ 56

Pressure .................................................................................... 59

**Chapter Three Social Perspectives** ........................................ 63

Hear Me Now ........................................................................... 63

Uncomfortable .......................................................................... 66

Prudence ................................................................................... 68

War or Peace ............................................................................. 71

We Stand Divided ..................................................................... 73

I'll Never Forget ....................................................................... 75

Misunderstood .......................................................................... 79

Human Labels ........................................................................... 82

One Nation Under God ............................................................. 86

A Beautiful Masterpiece ........................................................... 88

**Chapter Four Divine Inspiration** ........................................... 91

A Conversation With God ........................................................ 91

The Enemy Of Faith ................................................................. 95

We Confuse Greatness With Folly ........................................... 98

The Qualms of Mystery .......................................................... 101

Pro God, Pro Gun, Pro-Life .................................................... 104

Through the Lens of One Greater ........................................... 108

| | |
|---|---|
| Why Do The Religious Disagree? | 111 |
| From Fear to Faith | 114 |
| A Priceless Jewel Unseen | 116 |
| We Cannot Stay Here! | 119 |

# Chapter One
# Personal Reflection

## Hurt Beyond Words

If only I knew
What survives
Beneath the feelings
Of my heart,
An unmovable
Sensation,
From endless pain
That dictates
My inability
For affection.


Similar to one
Suffocating
In a house on fire,
As the smoke squanders
Every chance
To breathe,
Like being trapped
With no hope,
Consumed

By thoughts
Of being burned alive.


Though
The words
Seem so far away,
As I attempt
To describe
What I see
From a distance,
A heavy fog that blocks
My vision,


So I'm unable to discern
Threats
Designed my way.
For each day
I'm speechless
About what to say.


Like a muzzle
Forced upon my mouth,
The silence
Tortures my spirit,
As I run from
The shadows,
Consumed

By my decay.
Now I see images
In my peripheral
That appear real.
Within the confinements
Of my wounded mind,
I feel deceived


By hidden confusion,
So difficult
To perceive,
My hurt
Beyond words,
And long silent cries.

# In Weakness

I despise myself
Whenever I concede
To the powers within
That wage war
Against my core,
Making me doubt
All progress gained,
Only to agonize
In insecurity,
As one frail
And confused.

Wondering
Why have I
Abandoned
Everything I trust,
For a moment
Of pleasure,

To scourge myself
By the benefit
That comes
From resistance,
During trials
When motives
Are examined
And defined.

I can now recognize
The tactics
Of my opposition,
Deceptive
And conniving,
Like a rival at war
That evaluates
Its subjects,

To devour and conquer
Until a surrender
Is forced against
Their will.

Though I am weak,
I have learned
Knowledge
That has prolonged
My campaign
To inspire
Ambition,
Not just to survive
But to combat my foe
Both seen
As well as unseen,
To change
The narrative
In my life,
Before my end
Is certain.

# Criticism at Close Range

Why is everything
I've decided to pursue
Scrutinized?
Similar to a person
Choosing their own way
On a new project
Or job to complete,
When it's
Never good enough,
And your feelings
Of failure

Force you to examine
What has happened
Over the years,
As dreams
Get buried
Beneath every fear,
To cope with truths
You can't even hear.

Though,

Many questions
Plague my mind,
With years of doubt
From all my steps

Being criticized,
Like a warrior
Hunted
By a skilled assassin
In a hostile land,
Who waits
For his victims
To expose
Their faults,
So he can
Shoot them down,
Again and again.

Therefore,
I ponder
How one
Can have progress
In a world,
When reputations
Are defined
By misfortune,
Failures,
Wasted efforts,
And skewed
Perspectives?
Only to realize
They've been
Stained
By anguish,

From the perils
Of their inability
To grasp concepts
Outside their capacity.

Furthermore,
I'm unaware
Of my feelings,
When compared
To people
Whose lives
Are never respected,
That transcend
Negativity
By way

Of their actions,
Corrupt ideals,
And coveted
Unhealthy views,

Who justify others
For personal
Appeasement
By hollow praise.

And lastly,
I hope
My folly

Will not be my end,
When criticism

At close range

Comes from within.

# Impulse

Why do I
Get excited
By things I desire
Or cannot have,
While some days
Flirt with the idea
Of something new,
Thinking it will
Be sensational,
Then forgetting

The consequences
For what I do.

Like the feeling

Of an emotional high,
For an instance
So indescribable

It's easy to think why.
I convince myself further
To entertain the lie,
That my actions
May be worth
The effort and time,
But I must not
Forget,
It's an impulse

With a reputation,

That thrives

In trickery

And loves to hide.

# The Wall

In the distance

I can see

The magnitude
Of a great wall,
That appears
Impossible to climb,
Built by a force
Unknown,
With a threat
Beyond my reality,
Birthed
In the core

Of my thoughts,
Like a chasm
Similar
To the difference
Between
Rich and poor.

I felt overwhelmed
As I fell
Onto the floor,
By the wall
In my view

Never seen before.

Therefore,
As I thought
To myself,
If only I had
The experience
Or skill to achieve
What appears
Unreachable,
While I grapple
With infinite time
During the days
Of my restless life,
Fueled by confidence
And inspired dreams,
To have
A special talent
To climb
By all means.

In retrospect,
When I look
Within the depths
Of my heart,
My challenges

Appear hopeless,
Like a disabled man
Controlled and haunted
By habitual fears,
Unable to reach

Each step,

As his end

Draws nearer,

Only to entertain

A fancy

Instead of a dream,

That requires

Tenacity,

Ambition,

Commitment,

And broken tears,

To one day

Climb the wall

He has always feared.

# Risk It All

Can I face

An impossible dare
In order to embrace change

To secure my victory?
When the drive
That lives inside
Is like a passion, consumed

As a fire,
Built up
By simple suspicion
And pride
I cannot hide.

Just like

A daredevil
Who profits from the thrill
To live or die,
Who sails over barriers
In the sky so high,

That only his skill
Will determine his fate

For a stunt so great,
As he conquers
All odds

To overcome defeat.

In essence,
Courage lives
Within the heroes
We hear about and see,
Who face failure
Every day
Regardless of their deeds,

As truth and lies
Are disguised in their way.
Great plans
Can seem irrational
When it's time

For a chance
To one day
Risk it all.

# The Mystery Man

It seems serious
When people

First glance
Upon this man,
Like a blackout
In a major city
With no power
To do anything,
But wait until
The lights
Come back on again.

Then fear

Adopts the nature
Of some,
When confronted
With their new vision,
A dark man
In proximity.
So I watch
With anticipation
And ask

Only one question…
Why all
The strange looks,
Like a tragedy

Of innocent men,
Overshadowed
By media cases
Involving crimes
Of unarmed faces?

Though
It doesn't
Stop there,
'Cause people
Say crazy things, like:
"You live here?"
And "Wow,
You speak well."

So I ponder,
Just to say,
I must be unique,

Always thinking compliments,
Never perceiving insults.
But today,

That's all changed,
'Cause now I can see…
This mystery man
Is me.

# The Hardest Path

When I begin my journey,

I desire peace

Without the terror

Of infamy,

As I forge forward

Upon my quest

For destiny.

Though the way

Of the great

May be filled

With obstacles

Like thorns and bristles,

Or ridicule intended for blame.

As fame

Can sometimes be defined

By the result

Of one's shame,

That succumbs

To powers

Not yet seen.

Therefore,

The vision of the ambitious

Is embedded through resolve,

When they accept

Every intuition

In their drive
For completion,

As they walk

Fearlessly in bravery
On the hardest path
Of destiny.

# The Uncertainty of Everything

Honestly,

I hate how I feel,
Inspired to execute,
Determined to succeed,
But afflicted by worry
About health
And unfinished deeds.

Like finally having peace
Only to be displeased,
By the storms of anxiety,
From an inability
To breathe.

Therefore,

I long to behold
The efforts
Of my labor,

Like fruit when it's ripe,
That started as a seed.
Though skepticism
Prods me
To the edge
Of insanity,

As the invisible enemy
Shows me no mercy.
So I question myself…

Will I ever be sure
About the vision
Of my dreams?

For each step
I take in life
Is like a scary walk
Across a dangerous high beam,
That intensifies my core
To further explore,

Though

Only momentarily,

As I deem to untangle
Every trap of duplicity,
Like the uncertainty
Of everything,

That makes me
Unstable.

# Forever

I feel as though
A dark cloud
Hovers over me,

Like a thick mist
That seizes my mind,
Where emotions
Have no description,
Words are absent,
And the process
Seems impossible

For me to express
The true condition
Within my heart.

For it was

An unexpected shock
In my family,
As death attacked
Once again,
Like a tornado
Whistling in the night.

The son of my sister
Dropped dead,
In a hospital bathroom,
From an enlarged heart
At the age of 23,

Right before her eyes,

As her tears
Never stopped flowing
Like a waterfall
Out of control.

As the pain
Within her heart
Went deep

Into her soul.

In contrast,

I have learned

From his life and death
That it's not
How much I say

In this world that matters,
But how many
People I love.

As fate
Is the eternal result
Of all mankind,
For it confronts
Our sanity
And incites our courage

To accept the process
Of extinction
Before the powers

Unknown…
When alone,

Forever.

# Chapter Two
# Imaginary Expression

## Good Tree, Bad Tree

If I were a tree,
Would I have
The option
To be planted
In an environment
Where I could grow
And be free?


Just think of the trees
That we observe
Every day,
How beautiful
The leaves,
And unique
In strength.


Though at times
Unable
To truly perceive
Danger,

By catastrophe,
The incubator
Of disease.


With insect
Infestation,
And starvation
From a lack
Of nutrients,
Damage
Is created

By all means.


Therefore,
I must consider…
What kind of tree
Would I be
If that were me,
With no power
To choose,
Situations
Outside my control?


Like the poor
And unprivileged
That we judge
Every day,

Not understanding
The meaning
Behind the scenes
Of their poverty.


When we decide
To walk away
Only to avoid
Their needs.


Though daily,
We are exposed
When we face
Adversity,
Which provides
Insights
And factors
That reveal
The fruit
On a good or bad tree.

# I Saw Two Dragons

I couldn't believe

What devoured

My mind,

When worry

Within my soul

Began to intensify,

Similar

To a tragedy


In a peaceful home,

Where violence builds,

And the truth

Cannot hide,

Like the sight

Of two

Fire-breathing dragons,

Attacking a city

In the blink of an eye.


In my unconscious

State of mind,

I witnessed

Two dragons

In my dream.

So, I made every effort

To run away,
Though trapped
Was the feeling
Brewing inside.


Like an insect
Twisted
In a spider's web,
Trying to survive.


Meanwhile,
As I watched
Parts of buildings fall,
With large amounts
Of debris,
Like plastic
Marred in flames,
Never to be occupied
Or viewed the same.


Then I woke,
Frantically
From the deep
Of my sleep,
Perplexed and panicked
By what I had seen,

A vision so real
It frightened me.



So, I refused
To understand
The meaning
Of this nightmare
In my dream,
As paralysis


Quenched
My spirit
And devoured
My courage
By all means.


In the end, I pondered
The purpose
Of this horrific revelation,
Consumed
By images
That disturbed


My thoughts
And sanity,

About two

Fire-breathing dragons

Causing chaos

In my dream.

# Dark Eyes

As people walk by
During the peak
Of the day,
I see their reflection,
Very subtle and bleak.


Even though
They believe
Their pain
Is not visible


Or obvious to see,
The dark eyes
Of the living
Don't appear
To be free.


When I look


Into their eyes,
I see a deep
Darkness,
Similar to the night,
Like the abuser

Who is tormented
By their actions,
For not living
Right.


Just like an addict
In panic,
Who seeks
Their next fix,
With dread
On their faces,
Disrupted
In mysticism,
By forces
And misery
Unknown.


Furthermore,
They appear
To be held


As prisoners
In captivity,
By a ruthless,
Destructive enemy,
Not wanting them
To find

The secret

For sanity,

To cure

Their damaged mind.

Therefore, I wonder…

Is it bitterness

That grips the soul

Of people living

In bondage?

Or a spirit of hate

That betrays

The heart,

From people

Once trusted,

Like family

And friends?

In conclusion,

Could it be

The same people

Who offended
The innocent
For many years?


As the shadows
Linger
Upon the victims
With dark eyes,
Controlled
By demons


And a broken will.

# The Fierce, Tenacious, and Ordinary

There once lived a
King,
Who displayed courage
Beyond the norm
Of humanity,


Who conquered worlds
From journeys unknown,
And displayed


A vigor for victory,
Unmatched
By his foe.


Though,
The king hated
Being average.
He viewed
Mediocrity
As a tragedy,


So he burned
Within his soul,
While tormented

About growing old.

He faced mortality
With great strength,
Sharing stories
Never told.

First,

There are a few
Who demonstrate
A fierce attitude

To dominate
In the midst
Of extreme adversity,
Like a warrior
That perceives
Threats
As a routine epiphany.

Certain
Every challenge
Is worth the cost
For dignity,

Despite
All odds,
Responsible
For the epitome
Of defeat.


Secondly,
There are some
Who are tenacious,
Firm and unwavering,


From obstacles
That divert their path
For destiny.


Like a lion
In the desert,
Who conquers
His prey,
As starvation
Is never an option.


So he refuses
To stay
In a land

Without resources
For the rest
Of his days.


Likewise,
The lion
Will even search
For other prey—
Rodents, reptiles,
And other animals—
By adapting
In new ways,
To dominate
The land
With tenacity
While he rules
As king.


In contrast,
There are people
Who live
Ordinary lives,
That speak
Of many dreams
But never
Pursue them,
Because their energy
Is given to waste.

Like the consumption
Of foods
Without nutrients,
That decrease
Personal development,
Affect
Bodily functions,
And increase
Vulnerability
To disease.


Likewise,
They live
In terror,
Like cowards
At war,
That constantly
Avoid conflict
And never explore.


But sabotage
Themselves
By doubts and blame,
While living
Just to survive,
Without ambition

To truly change.

# Worthy

There was a woman
That lived
With a man
Who was deranged.


And every day
When he
Yelled at her,
She would cry
From his mind games.


Though,
The man
Looked
Like a cup
That was clean
On the outside,
But inside,
His demeanor
Was consumed
With rage
And multiple lies.

Similarly,

He would boast
About his love,
But only
In violent ways.


For his actions
Mirrored crimes
That always

Ended in remorse.


This man
Would always
Say, "I'm sorry,"
And follow
With this phrase…

*"Baby, you know I love you."*

But the torment
Would never change.


Similar

To daily torture
On a prisoner's
Forehead
During wartime,

By a faucet
Of dripping water,
That makes one
Lose their way.

Only to be made
More fragile,

As a victim

From dominance
And horrific fear.

Though
This woman
Would cry
For many
More years.

Still broken
And unloved,
She fought back
From within,
To regain

Her inner strength,
To forgive
What he did.

In her mind,
She proclaimed
Freedom,
Like a slave
Unleashed,
To finally see
Her value
As a woman,
Truly worthy.

# The Mother, Father, and Wife

I can't imagine

The anguish

One must feel,

To lose three people

In a year,

When life

Was consumed

With peace, laughter,

Love, and then despair,

Only to experience

Moments

Filled with many tears.


Like a dam

That breaks

In your presence

Way before its years,

That traumatizes

Your reality

By an endless

Mystified stare.


First,

There was the mother

Who molded
Her son,

Like a bear
That protects
Her cubs,
To train them
For efficiency,
In a dangerous,
Dark, and frigid world.

Ultimately,
Her love for him
Was priceless,
Like a beautiful
Special pearl.

Then, mysteriously,
She began to lose
Her mind,
From memory loss
Every day,
As her life ended
In the nick of time,
Before her son
Could even pray.

Secondly,

There was his father

Whose character

Was defined

By brilliant design.

While poised

In honor

And intellect,

He supplied

His only seed

For his one

And only son…

An absolute

Treasure indeed.


Likewise,

The father was

A mirror image

Of his son,

With patience

And wisdom

Unmatched.


As the years

Passed by,

Like sand

Dripping in a glass,

His father
Suddenly died
From a stroke
Before he gasped
His final breath.


And lastly,

The son had
A wife
That he truly,
Deeply loved,
Who was vibrant
In her presence…
Which was obviously
From above.


As a woman,

She had compassion
And displayed
Relentless love,
Not just for him
But for others.
Her motives
Were pure,
Like a dove.

Moreover,
Her legacy
Required attention,
Like an eclipse
Embedded
In the sky.

Her radiance
Was bright
With reflection,
A gift
He couldn't deny,

Even though,

In the end,
It was cancer
That took her
By God's side.

# The Foe Living Within

It feels like a boulder
That appears
Unmovable,
As it destroys
All hope,
By schemes
Ployed
With frustration

When absent of noise.


In contrast,
It's like living
Consumed
In a world
Of personal void,
Unable to conquer
The vile,
Breathing noise
That lives within,

With weapons
So subtle,
Like the calm
Before a storm,
That never
Seems to end.

Additionally,
As one fights
To live a legacy
Of victory
And not defeat,
The enemy
Longs to watch
The downfall
Of everyone
He meets.


Like a champion
In crisis,
Not knowing
The cost
Or value
Of what's been lost,
From the effects
For years,
In silent destruction,
By the foe
No one sees…
Living within.

# The Crumbs of Life

The crumbs
We see
Before our eyes
Are similar
To the aroma
That never
Seems to die.
As it constantly
Exists in our midst,
While some
Choose to deny,
And others,
Filled with hunger,
Search for the bits
Which have fallen
Onto the ground.


In contrast,
When the crumbs
Are discovered
On the floor,
A dog will track
His provisions,
With ambitious
Anticipation,
Like a new treat

For the very

First time,

Making him desire

The scraps

More than before.


Though,

The crumbs

Of one's life

Could be

The prize

That changes

A person's fortune,

When pursued

By ambition

As well as

Humility.


So they may learn

What they never

Knew before…

That crumbs

Are a delicacy

For the rich

And the poor.

# A Wild Horse

People feared this animal

Based on

Its behavior,

As it would buck

And fight,

Whenever others approached

Or got close.

For the bronco

Was highly intelligent,


Though no one understood why


The horse


Was so disobedient,

Like a defiant menace

In our community,

Making all who observed

Conclude,

"The horse is crazy

And unreachable."


As the days passed by,

A horse whisperer

Came into town
And was told everything
About the wild horse.
So, he went to the stalls
To approach
The wild, rebellious beast
Everyone feared.


Though, he was not afraid.

When he met the horse,
He approached
According to its ways,

Showing it patience,
Love,
And understanding,
Like a mother
With a wild child,
Causing it to cease.


In retrospect,
We all recall
Meeting a wild horse—
Someone who's been hurt,
Abused,
And, worst-case scenario,
Abandoned

During his or her youth.

Causing anger,

Insecurity,

And fear,

Which does not define them,

But creates

A false narrative

Others believe,

From their perspective…

To avoid or give up

On the wounded,

Scarred souls

In our society.

# Pressure

Have you ever
Felt the burdens
Of life come down

On you, all at once?

Like a pile of rocks
Being thrown
In your face,
Beyond rage,
For an offense,

Recorded for years,

Compiled as evidence
Against you?

As a result,
This describes
The epitome
Of my current situation,
Like a detour
At night,

When your gas

Is low,

In an unknown
Neighborhood,
Damaged by a storm.


With fallen trees
Everywhere,
And many
Destroyed homes,
Where darkness
Ruled the land,
With no power
To restore.


I could only wait
In anticipation,
As despair
Increased more.


Though,
My quest
For answers
Continued,
Like a miner
Searching for gold.

Therefore,

I asked myself
Two questions:

First,
Can I handle
The pressure
That threatens
All parts
Of my soul?

Secondly,
Will I rise
Past my potential
As a man
Who learns
The essence
Of leadership
In his home?

And not be
A fragile man,
Defined by madness
When alone.

# Chapter Three
# Social Perspectives

## Hear Me Now

They claim to be of power

But use others for blame,

Though their lives

Seem to differ

From the common American way.


For criticalness, lies,

And slander

Travel in their veins,

As these imposters

Cling to false truth

Not yet examined

From their expensive campaigns.


Easily deceiving

A country that still remains,

Mesmerized by riches,

Vomiting ideas and politics

With fictitious claims,

Only to be accepted

By mutual thinkers

Who know not

Our nation's pain.


Within their circle
Of friends and foes,
Two parties
Fight and disagree
About the needs and lives
Of people unseen.


Though blatantly
They expose
Our country's shameful ways,
By closing their ears
And hiding their eyes,
They fail to recognize
We're all humans
Trying to survive.


Like a passing of the wind
Drifting aimlessly
In the brisk of day,
Confusion
Conditions the minds
Of those slipping away.


By agitators on the rise,

Unwilling to change,
Opinions so toxic,
Even the crazy
Appear sane.


Consequently,
The oppressor
Shuts the door
On those deserving a chance…
For justice, prosperity,
And truth behind the lies.


Therefore, we stand,
As one people
Of all kinds,
Never to forget…
America is not for trade.


Hear me now!
Oh, hear me now!
Before life
Is not the same.

# Uncomfortable

Conflict
Is not the end of all things
But the beginning.


For some, discomfort
Becomes an opportunity
To quit or run away,
Though the courageous
Challenge to captivate
And start anew,
In a different way.


At times,
The wounds
Caused by words
Can build prisons
That always remain.


Friends and families
Have disagreements,
Creating chasms every day,
Like being exiled
From your community,
Knowing you can't stay.

So why give
A life sentence
To the ones you love,
Who oppose
What you say?


Like issues we debate
Related to societal trends
That threaten
What we've built over time…
From narrow thinking
And biased perspectives,
Year after year.


As a result,
Some contend to behave
Like spoiled children,
Who scowl and scream
When they don't get their way,
While feeling uncomfortable
For the rest of their days.

# Prudence

Be silent in a room
Filled with loud talkers,
And they will look upon you
With great anticipation,
To hear your opinion.


Whenever
You are in the heat
Of an argument,
Choose to be quiet
In your position,
And think before you speak,
To calm the anger
Of your adversary,
Like the peace
That comes at the end
Of a storm.


Similar to the end
Of a major earthquake,
Is the result
For those who find relief
In the form of justice,
When they've been
Citizens for years,

Overshadowed
By a system
Built on bribes.


Just like
Lying and deceit
Are no different
From hypocrisy and corruption,
Both evils
Depend on actions
Promoted in secret.


As a result,
Living every day
To gain satisfaction
From prestige and popularity
Is a waste of life
When you never
Reach your destiny.


Furthermore,
If you disagree
With the politics
Of another person,
But have no answers
To combat their opinion,
Keep it to yourself

Until you gain more knowledge,
So you may secure
Your civic position.


In essence,
When two hostile individuals
Brew their disgust
In the heat of an argument,
They reveal
Emotional immaturity,
Displaying the epitome
Of recklessness
And personal defeat.


In the short term,
People who do wrong
May get away with it
For the moment,
But in the end,
They will receive
What they plant
In the minds
Of those who listen,
With an unfavorable return.

# War or Peace

Is not war inescapable,
With threats so appealing,
It provokes our pride
While living within
The fears of victimization?


As the strong linger
For a chance
To conquer and divide,
Every spoil from victory
Tempts us all to deny
Offensive reactions
Beyond comprehension
And private demise.


Though peace
Is the aroma of war,
And at times, impossible
To attain…
At the brink of insanity
And vague despair.


Especially
During moments
That define

All boundaries,
Never to be crossed,
If indeed you cared
About the luxury
Of absolute harmony…
A gift in this world
For those who beware.


The recklessness of war
Before it begins
Like a terror.

# We Stand Divided

Are you an American
Confused
By media outlets
Presenting their views?


Do you believe the news?


Nobody knows
What to believe
From the right,
Or what is discussed
On the left,
As both agendas
Have trapped our minds
To excuse this mess.


Dressed up by biases
On each side of the aisle,
It's hard to listen to the noise
That torments our lives,
While shredding our spirit
To enjoy being an American.


This has pushed us to the edge,

With dreams placed on delay.


Like a fortified army
On both sides of a wall,
Standing toe to toe,
Not understanding the cost…
Neither side budging
To listen or comply.


Divided we stand,
And together we fall.


Today,
If we refuse
To look back and reflect,
We will lose
Perspective.


History reminds us all…
Every great nation
Can one day fall
When it dies
From the inside,
By corruption and lies.

# I'll Never Forget

During most days
Of my life,
I despised
The heritage
Of my ancestors…
For reasons
Without merit,
Knowledge,
Or validity.


The stains
Embedded by ignorance
Influenced shame
Beyond reason.


Though,
As I matured
Through life,
The sentiments
In my perspective
Affected my heart,
Like an ambush
Or raid—
A misplaced assault
On vulnerable nations.

Only to be caught
And abused
For profit
By those in power,
Who displayed
Not a hint of dignity.


In retrospect,
How can one hate
The pure essence
Associated with their
Innate being,
When unaware
Of the brutal impact
Caused by atrocities?


Forced upon a people
Who once lived
Lives of freedom
And prosperity,
Only to be taken
By those empowered
To remove all humanity.


Within a political realm
That promoted

The exploitation
Of human beings.


Today,
I will never forget
My ancestry,
Nor the painful truth
Associated with
Civil disobedience
Recorded in history.


Of those misunderstood
And used to defame…
People like me,
In a land not their own.


Who remain strangers,
After centuries,
Only to be mocked
To appease those
Who hid their corruption
By profiting
On the efforts
Of people dehumanized.


Whose blood, death,

And names are unknown.

# Misunderstood

How can humanity
Be villainized,
While being a victim
To oppressors,


Who govern nations
And set boundaries
Where people
Are forced to dwell,
Within confinements
Of an obscure territory,
Imposed upon a society
Without reason or say,
As the crying souls
Have been misplaced
From their
Inhabited land today.


In retrospect,
When I listen
To the viewpoint
As well as the narrative
Of the news,
It's extremely biased
Toward one group

And opposes
The other,
Like marginalization
For certain people,
Where media skews
Our perception
And affects reality
Common to all,
Who claim
To understand,
But fail to recognize
Brutality disguised,
By justification
For actions unseen.


Lastly, I heard
Three dozen
Christians died,
Who lived in the land
We claim to despise,
With cries unheard.
I didn't realize

Their unknown faces
As well as lives,
While many religious
In my country
Seem paralyzed,
For trauma imposed

On our chosen enemy.


Are we not
Desensitized

By propaganda
And a lack
Of human dignity?
Or are the people
In that land
Just misunderstood?

# Human Labels

Why do we
Label people
And despise
Everything
About them,
By creating
Filtered narratives
Against
Groups of people?


Refusing
To change
Our personal view
While feeling justified
In behavior.


As a result,
A common hypocrisy
That lives
With us today,
Covered up
By pretentious
Discrimination
And blame,
For others' actions

When we
Do the same.


Consequently,
The worst offenders
Involve those
With great claims,
Whose lives
Don't honor His name,
Professing love
While heaping abuse
And
Inciting hate
On all groups,
Increasing their shame.


We label people
As Black, White, Hispanic,
Asian, Indian, and the like,
Only to rationalize
Reasoning


For prejudgment,
To demoralize
What we choose
Not to identify
Or like,

And hide hostile
Accusations
In our minds,
About those
Different than our kind.


Furthermore,
We justify

Why we oppose
Christians, Muslims,
Catholics, Homosexuals,
Lesbians, Transgenders,
Racists, Republicans,
Democrats,

And anyone else
That doesn't agree,
With the human labels
In society
We've created,

Not to defend or see.


In essence,
Love is the response
To our global
Social problem,
If only we viewed
People as humans

And not
Another label,
But sought
To understand
The why
Behind the motives
Of a person
In every human label.

# One Nation Under God

If God judged us
As a nation,
Would we care
For each other more,
Rather than
Despise mankind,
When we see acts
That violate

Our moral minds?
Or will we love
Even though
We don't

Fully understand
We're all connected,
Through one man
Who chose
To shed His blood
So we could stand
United in His plan?


Unfortunately,
I think
Many can't see it,
Because they seek
Their own glory

And not He,
Who created
The world
Not to abuse,
But to walk justly
With humility
And embrace
Mercy for every race.


So people
In every tribe,
Language, and nation,
Will not destroy
One another,
By repeating history
From the ignorance
Instituted
Through racism and pride
On both sides.


I wonder
If our country survives,
As one nation under God.

# A Beautiful Masterpiece

When I observe
Paintings,
I long to view
A masterpiece,
That exemplifies
An essence
Of multiple colors,
In harmony
Whether dark or light,
With intriguing
Endless emotions,
Profound uniqueness,
Powerful stillness,
Compelling disposition,
Vibrant harmony,
And delicate hidden
Visual perspectives.


This artistic piece
Compels all
To wonder
Based upon
The brilliance,
Intelligence,
Experience,
Reputation,

And genius,
Of the artist at work,
Whose mind
Is never dull,
But thrives
In complexity,
As well as vision.


What is it
That I see
From my eyes?
But a masterpiece
Of the sky,
Covered in shades
Like blue, grey, orange,
Black, and white,
With clouds
So transparent,
They present
A magnificent sight,
Only to be seen
By those
Who look up
And cry,
Saying,

*"Why all these years*
*Have I chosen*
*To deny*

*Other humans*
*By my racial pride?"*


In essence,
We are all a part
Of this masterpiece
In the history of art,
Just like nations
And civilizations,
That have existed
Over time,
Created in many colors
With the intention
To blend and unify,
Though resistance
Has been the habit
Not to comply
But divide.


For this artist's
Intention
Was to amaze
The color blind,
With colors
Beautifully blended,
According to His mind.

# Chapter Four
# Divine Inspiration

## A Conversation With God

*Yahweh,*

Please hear me.
Why is this life so hard?


I feel at times
That my efforts are futile,
And my belief wavers
From confusion,
Based on reasons misunderstood,
About the essential importance
Of living life to the full,
When burdened
By a heap of disappointment.


Today, as I wait
In anticipation,
I hear a voice saying,

*"Your life*
*Is unsatisfying because*
*It's based*
*On what you desire,*

*And not Me.*
*Remember*
*That freedom*
*Comes from Me,*
*Rather than your*
*Selfish ambition*
*To acquire peace,*
*Prosperity, and glory,*
*Which are nothing*
*For Me to provide.*
*Did I not create you*
*And all things?"*


Truly,

I do not know
How to respond
To Your truth,
As I strive
For a life of success,
Though frustrated
By the process.


I'm discouraged
By the roadblocks
Designed in my path,
Like a maze
That has no end.

Therefore, I question
Your support
Once again,
Only to find myself
Perplexed,
By situations
Beyond my control.

*Yahweh,*

How am I
To live in this world,
As a man
Who wants more
Out of life,
But has lost sight
Of Your ways,
From years of folly
And broken dreams?

That I've
Refused to face,
Only to realize
This journey
Is not my own,
Just like this world
Will never be

My home,
But a place
Filled with disparity.

# The Enemy Of Faith

You can't see it,
But it's there,
Breathing silently
Like an insane
Spiritual parasite,
In the crevices
Of the dark,

With a mission
To conquer life,
Like a predator
In the calm
Of the night,

Who doesn't care
About feelings
Or emotions,
Only to annihilate
Your confidence.


So beware.


Likewise,

This enemy hurls
Ruthless threats,
Seeking lives

On the fringes
Of reality,

While they dominate
The cowardly
By dismay, doubt,
And evil thoughts,
That enslave
Like a trap or snare,

With intentions
To make them captive
For the rest
Of their days.


In conclusion,

This adversary
Holds hostage
Every spirit,
As it instigates
Dreadful images,
Used as hidden
Propaganda,

Implanted within
The restraints
Of a wayward
Person's mind,

To sway
Their conviction

From core values,
As it casts
Never-ending attacks
On one's life.


For the enemy described
Is fear.

# We Confuse Greatness With Folly

If God is so great,
Why do people
Lie and deceive,
With an ambition
Not to be found out,
But desire
To make others
Believe they are good,
While hiding behind
Religion,

As they claim
How much
They love Jesus?


People,

Are you still so dull
That you're incapable
Of personal discernment?


Why not
Examine your life
And time,
Devoted
To self-appeasement,
While you rob God,

Whom you claim to follow,
By your ambition
For self-glory?


Our Creator,

In heaven and on earth,
Knows all things.


He is not unaware
Of our practices
Nor ambitions
To be recognized
By all,

Though many
People's hearts
And motives
Are absent
Of God's
Ways and principles,

As some are unaware
They testify against Him
By their own words.


Today,

Do you not hear
What you've said to others?

Can you not see
How you've treated
Other people?

For the living God
Is not to be mocked,
Nor misrepresented
In any way.

Therefore,

Get on your knees
And cry out to Him,
Proclaim to God
All truths
About your evil ways,

That forgiveness
May be the foundation
To radically transform
The remainder
Of your days.

# The Qualms of Mystery

It takes deep belief
In God,
To humble yourself
Before Him,

As you wait
With great anticipation
For God to act
Upon your request.


Though,

There are some
Who embrace pride
When they pray,
Like the power
Derives from them
Every day,

But fail to see
Their personal
Deception,
That makes life
A stumbling block,
In the channels
Of absolute faith.

Furthermore,

I wonder
Why mankind
Is so vain,
That he doubts

The validity
Of God's competency
To deliver
A petition of prayer
Dressed with tranquility?


And is mankind
Motivated
By the persistence
Of dignity?


For the diligent
And courageous
Reap and sow
Tests over time,
That defeat
The weak,
But fashion the strong,

Like the value
Of a plant
Embracing adversity,
By the depths of its roots

During the qualms
Of mystery.

# Pro God, Pro Gun, Pro-Life

I couldn't believe it
When I saw
This phrase
With my own
Two eyes,

A statement so bold
On a T-shirt,
For all to conceptualize,
The promotion
Of God, guns, and life,

A conflicting message
That gives birth
To strife,
In a nation
That remains disunified,
By the far left
And far right.


Certainly,

I agree,
The promotion
Of God is right,
For His sovereignty
Over creation,
Stretches

Beyond the earth,
Universe,
And mankind's strength,

Who continues
To be oblivious
By his pride,
Before he falls
Like stars
In the night,
Only to be led
By a spirit
Not from God.


In accordance,

I do agree,
Owning a gun
Has its privileges
For both
You and me,

Like the protection
Of oneself, family,
And friends.


Although,

I ponder
If Jesus

Would preach
This is right,
As He taught
To turn
The other cheek,
And to love
Our enemies,

So they can seek,
A power
Much greater,
Than you or me.


For example,

I heard a story
About ruthless thugs,
Robbing homes
From one of
The countries
In Africa,

Who came
To a woman's house,
Armed with guns,
With intent to kill,
Until they found
Her praying,
Not for herself,
But for them.

Then all
The thugs left,
By the power
Of her prayer.

In conclusion,
As I reflect
On the issue
Of power
Over death,
I cannot deny
That God
Gives freedom
For all
To decide,
Whether wrong
Or right,
While some
Tend to avoid
God's eternal
Consequences,
When faced
With a dilemma,
To choose
Another life.

# Through the Lens of One Greater

How do you view mankind?

Is your perception

Skewed by tragedy,

Unfortunate news,

And misconceptions based on fear…

From horrible experiences

That only you can see?


And when,

In the company of others,

What do you see?

Is it a world consumed with filth,

Or a beautiful rendition of the earth,

Molded by greater hands

Than you and me?


For the love of most

Appears to be absent,

And in most cases,

Non-existent.


So how are humans

To love unconditionally?

Is it not through
The eyes of the beholder
Who created all things?


So why be a hostage,
Controlled by personal bondage,
Only to lose sight…
To learn the true meaning
Of love,
For your enemies,
Accusers,
Strange outcasts,
And wicked, ruthless people,
Who despise proof
That God has created everything you see?


Furthermore,

As I read inspired scripture
About love,
Which states,
That whoever does not love,
Is not one who knows God,
Because Yahweh is love.


Therefore,

How can people

Claim to know Him,
But forfeit their efforts
Based upon hidden strongholds…
Of hate, exclusion,
And hypocrisy?


By acting godly,
While denying the reliance of His power…
To show kindness
In the way of His love.


Consequently,

Mankind must attain
A new worldview,
In order to see
Through the lens of Yahweh,
And love as He did,
Regardless of hurts, pains, worries,
And prejudgments,
That hinder the road
That leads to eternal life.

# Why Do The Religious Disagree?

Many people claim
To be right,
With arguments so convincing
It's hard to deny,
The reasons for their doctrine
And strong belief,
Just to be accepted,
Regardless of their lives.


Like an undercover cop
Deep in corruption,
Who breeds seeds of hypocrisy,
And continues to lie,
But desires to look good
Before the eyes of mankind.


Look,

It is the seed
That causes a church to divide,
Like the teachers of the law
Who hated Jesus…
The one they denied.


Just like churchgoers

Who always criticize
Any other movement
That conflicts with their kind,
But rarely
Can they see
Their own folly and shame.


Therefore,
I wait anxiously
For the day,
To witness unity
In those who proclaim,
Jesus as Lord
With their mouths and lives.


To one day die,
Conquer, and realize
Satan's brutal lies,
By the power of faith
In Jesus' holy name.


As one bold people,
That proudly unite
For His glory and fame.


Only to wait

In expectation,

As the end draws nearer.


I see darkness in fear,

Like a bully in shock,

By the coalition of us all,

Who fight to agree,

That Jesus is the way,

And not our prideful religious creeds,

So we may conquer

A fallen world,

In desperate spiritual need.

# From Fear to Faith

How can fear
Consume the appetite,
When real faith
Is the absent claim,
That many profess
To feel a sense
Of eternal security,
While they doubt
Their heavenly destiny?

From results
Consumed by anxiety,
And mental torment
Infused by the enemy.

Likewise,

Why is freedom
Jeopardized
By deceptive captivity?

That molds the unstable
To skew their heavenly perspective,
As it forges their steps
In uncertainty,

And breeds habits
Coerced in duplicity,
Only to be a victim for years
Of isolated suspicion.


Though,

Few have conquered
Their quest over fear,
To achieve dreams
Beyond the realm
Of what is unknown.


Thankfully,

The mystery
Has been answered,
By the resurrected King,
Whose disciples
Lived in terror,
For fear of death,
But later embraced
Courage to live,
Entrusted by faith,
With confidence to breathe
One last time.

# A Priceless Jewel Unseen

Recently,

I went to the doctor
For a CAT scan
Of my brain,
Because one morning,
I woke up,
With my arm and leg
Paralyzed
On my left side.

Though,

Fear dominated
The courage within my mind,
Like the thought
Of being absent from life
Without warning.

As insecurity became my face,
I was in shock,
By the depths of uncertainty.

In retrospect,

The only thing in this world
That matters

Is love.

For example,

When I spoke

To my sister,

She said,

*"God and we have you,*

*Regardless of the results."*

A confirmation

I needed to hear,

Which moved my heart

To an endless flow of tears.

In the end,

I must be aware

Of what I cannot see

From my eyes,

Or even hear

With my ears.

For unknown

Is the author,

Who endorses life

As well as death,

Only to be learned
By those who stop to see.


The brilliance in the sky,
Like a blue ocean at noon,
And a dark abyss
During the night.


While the wind blows
From left to right,
Just like God,
A priceless jewel unseen.

# We Cannot Stay Here!

Many live
With no worries or regrets,
As if death
Is not a reality,
Only to watch
Their proudest moments in life
Slip away.


Like homes
On a hillside,
Forced to move
By heavy rains,
Left for waste
And unusual decay.


So,
What will happen
To the arrogant
And boastful,
Who refuse to pray?


Will they cry out
In panic,
Not knowing what to say,

When death
Confronts them
Before their time?


Like the young,
Who vanish
Without a trace.


Is not,

What's unseen
More powerful
Than this place?


For who will seek
To learn
The Creator's ways?


As every day
Has been made,
Not to abuse
Or lose our way,
But to cherish
And honor.


Because tragedy

Can be unfortunate,
In a world
In which
We cannot stay.

www.ingramcontent.com/pod-product-compliance
Lightning Source LLC
LaVergne TN
LVHW020429070526
838199LV00004B/333